Original title:

Silent Revelations

Copyright © 2025 Swan Charm

All rights reserved.

Author: Kene Elistrand

ISBN HARDBACK: 978-1-80560-949-0

ISBN PAPERBACK: 978-1-80561-510-1

The Fire Beneath the Ashes

In shadows deep, where embers glow,
A whispered tale begins to flow.
With every spark, a story wakes,
From silent earth, the heart still aches.

Beneath the dust, a flame resides,
Unknown, yet felt, where hope abides.
It dances slow, yet burns so bright,
Illuminating the cloak of night.

The brittle past, like leaves, will rust,
But fire ignites forgotten trust.
In ashes rest, the dreams once lost,
Rekindled souls, no matter the cost.

Embrace the heat, let courage rise,
For in the heat, the spirit flies.
Through trials fierce, we find our way,
With every night, brings forth the day.

So let the fire guide our tread,
Through paths unmarked and futures spread.
For from the ashes, life will bloom,
And bask in warmth that conquers gloom.

Threads of Calm Truth

In silence woven, truth unfolds,
A tapestry of dreams, it holds.
With gentle hands, we stitch and mend,
The frayed edges, where we transcend.

Each thread, a story, soft yet strong,
A melody where hearts belong.
Through colors bright, our worlds align,
In patterns bold, our souls entwine.

As whispers linger in the air,
The essence of a love we share.
In every knot, a promise made,
In every space, no fear can invade.

Through trials faced, we travel far,
With every step, a guiding star.
The fabric holds, as life unfolds,
With threads of calm, we break the molds.

So let us weave with hearts sincere,
A bond unbroken, year by year.
In every thread, the truth we find,
A peaceful journey, intertwined.

Light Breaking Through

Soft rays dance on morning dew,
Gentle whispers of the new.
A world reborn, a vibrant hue,
Daylight's promise, fresh and true.

Shadows fade, they lose the fight,
Colors bloom in golden light.
Each moment rich, pure delight,
Hearts awaken, taking flight.

Clouds part ways, a clear blue sky,
Nature sings, a joyful cry.
Hope emerges, soaring high,
With each dawn, our spirits fly.

In this glow, we find our way,
Guided gently, come what may.
Together here, where dreams convey,
Light breaking through, a brand new day.

Silence as a Canvas

In tranquil stillness, thoughts take shape,
A quiet world, no need for escape.
Brush strokes soft, emotions drape,
In silence found, the heart's landscape.

Colors blend where shadows hide,
In muted tones, our dreams reside.
Each pause a moment, calm as tide,
On this canvas, we confide.

Words unspoken, yet understood,
Art of silence, rich and good.
Breaking barriers, as it should,
Creating peace in every wood.

A masterpiece of thought and air,
In stillness deep, we learn to care.
Through whispers soft, we lay it bare,
Silence molds the love we share.

The Gentle Unfolding

Petals slowly drink the sun,
A sacred dance, life has begun.
In every curve, a story spun,
Each breath a treasure, quietly won.

Moments linger, soft and sweet,
In nature's arms, we find our seat.
With every heartbeat, life's heartbeat,
The gentle unfolding feels complete.

Waves of time, like whispers sway,
In still embrace, we drift away.
Finding solace in the play,
Of gentle moments, day by day.

Nature hums its tender tune,
Beneath the watchful, silver moon.
In quiet grace, we're wrapped in boon,
The gentle unfolding, hearts attune.

Calm Horizons

Where the sky meets ocean's blue,
Waves of peace roll into view.
Endless dreams, horizons true,
In quiet moments, hearts renew.

Glimmers dance on the water's face,
Each swell a soft, warm embrace.
In whispered winds, we find our place,
Calm horizons, a sacred space.

Clouds drift slowly, time stands still,
In quietude, we seek our thrill.
With every breath, a gentle will,
Guiding souls to climb the hill.

As dusk descends, the stars awake,
In twilight's hush, the world we stake.
Together here, our bonds we make,
On calm horizons, love's heartache.

Whispers in the Void

In shadows deep, the silence hums,
Lost echoes dance where no light comes.
A breath of dusk, a fleeting sigh,
Whispers in the void, where dreams comply.

Stars will guide the wandering souls,
Through darkened paths, where time extols.
A gentle nudge, a hidden spark,
Illuminates the vast expanse, stark.

In whispered tones, the cosmos calls,
Beyond the void, where silence falls.
Forgotten tales that linger near,
Whispers softly fade, yet appear.

A fleeting touch, an ancient lore,
In every pulse, there's something more.
The cosmos speaks in muted tones,
In whispers' dance, we're not alone.

To lose and find in endless night,
In whispers flow, we seek the light.
In quietude, the heart may roam,
In whispers found, we'll find our home.

The Stillness Speaks

In tranquil hours, when shadows blend,
The stillness whispers, a quiet friend.
It holds the truth in gentle shades,
Where silence blooms, and doubt just fades.

With every breath, the moments pause,
In stillness wrapped, we find the cause.
A heartbeat echoes between the trees,
The stillness speaks in the evening breeze.

In soft retreat, the chaos clears,
The stillness hums, it calms our fears.
In every blink, a world anew,
Where quiet minds can see what's true.

As twilight falls, the colors merge,
In stillness found, our souls diverge.
A sacred space, where thoughts align,
In stillness dwells, the sacred sign.

The night unveils its starry art,
In stillness felt, we touch the heart.
Here in the calm, life's secrets unveil,
The stillness speaks, a soft, sweet tale.

Echoes of Inner Truths

In chambers deep, where whispers dwell,
Echoes linger, secrets swell.
Beneath the noise, the heart reveals,
The inner truths that time conceals.

With every thought, a ripple grows,
In silent depths, the insight flows.
A moment caught in stillness bright,
Echoes of truths bring forth the light.

In gentle waves, the past will call,
To hear the echoes, we mustn't stall.
They resonate through time and space,
Echoes linger, a warm embrace.

With courage found, we break the mold,
In echoes heard, our tales unfold.
With every step, we choose to see,
The echoes speak of who we'll be.

Within the depths, the journey starts,
In sacred echoes, we find our parts.
To honor those who came before,
Echoes of truths, forevermore.

Unvoiced Secrets

In shadows cast, where whispers creep,
Unvoiced secrets, in silence steep.
They weave a tale beneath the skin,
Where hidden realms of thoughts begin.

A glance exchanged, a fleeting spark,
In silent rooms, where echoes hark.
What's left unsaid, hangs in the air,
Unvoiced secrets linger everywhere.

Between the lines, the heart will know,
What's buried deep, may start to show.
In subtle signs, the truth shall find,
Unvoiced secrets, in heart and mind.

With gentle care, we tread the line,
To speak the words, to intertwine.
In every pause, there lies a key,
Unvoiced secrets that set us free.

So let us dare to share our plight,
To lift the veil, to grasp the light.
In every whisper, find the grace,
Unvoiced secrets, our sacred space.

Voices Lost in Time

Whispers echo through the years,
Forgotten tales, bound by fears.
In shadows deep, their stories lie,
Silent echoes of a sigh.

Faded laughter, distant cries,
Layered truths beneath the skies.
Fragments drift in twilight's glow,
Moments lost, yet all we know.

Pages worn from history's hand,
Legacy like shifting sand.
With every breath, we seek and yearn,
For voices past to teach and burn.

Yet in the dark, they softly call,
To break the silence—stand or fall.
Their lessons weave through time's embrace,
In every heart, they find a place.

So heed the echoes from afar,
A guiding light, a flickering star.
For in the loss, we learn to find,
The vibrant threads that bind mankind.

The Hidden Symphony

In whispers soft, the music plays,
Beyond the noise of bustling days.
A gentle breeze, a rustling leaf,
Nature's song, a sweet relief.

With every footstep on the ground,
A hidden rhythm can be found.
The trickle of a stream nearby,
A symphony to touch the sky.

In shadows cast by evening's glow,
Melodies begin to flow.
Each star a note, each moonbeam light,
Together crafting pure delight.

So pause a while, just close your eyes,
Let music bloom, let spirit rise.
For in the silence, sounds abound,
A fleeting world that knows no bounds.

The hidden notes in every heart,
Compose a song that won't depart.
With every beat, the truth will chime,
A harmony lost in time.

Serene Discoveries

Amidst the calm, the world reveals,
A gentle touch, a warmth that heals.
In quiet places, peace takes flight,
Softly glowing in the night.

The rustling grass, the evening breeze,
Whispering tales among the trees.
Hidden gems, both near and far,
Shimmer like a distant star.

In every droplet, life reflects,
Nature's love, its purest respects.
With every breath, we start to see,
The beauty woven into we.

Upon the hills, the sun descends,
A tranquil moment that transcends.
For in stillness, hearts align,
To find the light that brightly shines.

So venture forth, embrace the calm,
In every heartbeat, find the balm.
For every step, a chance awaits,
To uncover life's hidden gates.

The Language of the Unseen

In shadows where the silence dwells,
A language deeper than mere spells.
A glance, a smile, a tender touch,
In subtleties, we find so much.

The breeze that whispers through the trees,
Conveys a depth, a soulful tease.
In every pause, the stories bloom,
Beyond the noise, beyond the gloom.

With every heartbeat, we align,
Unspoken words that intertwine.
Though lips may seal, the heart can sing,
A symphony of everything.

Feelings shared without a sound,
In every moment, love is found.
Through eyes that shine and hearts that yearn,
In languages of love, we learn.

So listen close, to what is felt,
In every glance, emotions dealt.
For in the quiet, truth unfolds,
A timeless tale that never grows old.

Pondering in Peace

In the shadow of the trees,
Thoughts drift like autumn leaves,
Whispers of the gentle breeze,
Time flows with such sweet ease.

The world outside fades away,
As the heart begins to sway,
Each moment here will stay,
In quietude, I long to lay.

Beneath the sky so wide,
Nature's secrets, I confide,
In solitude, I bide,
With calmness as my guide.

Dreams emerge like evening stars,
Revealing old and hidden scars,
In the stillness, healing starts,
Each breath, a work of art.

Pondering here in peace,
Where all my worries cease,
In this moment, I find release,
In nature's tender fleece.

The Silence Sings

In the hush of twilight's glow,
Softly where the shadows grow,
Silent songs begin to flow,
Echoes of a heart's hello.

In the stillness, whispers weave,
Tales of love that never leave,
In the quiet, we believe,
The heart's rhythm, we receive.

Stars like notes in velvet night,
Sparkle softly, pure and bright,
In this space, we take flight,
With every breath, our spirits light.

Gentle tremors fill the air,
Moments woven, threadbare care,
In the silence, magic's fair,
Interwoven everywhere.

The silence sings a tune divine,
A melody that feels like time,
In the quiet, hearts entwine,
In peaceful shadows, love's design.

Quietude's Embrace

Wrapped in quietude's warm hold,
Stories of the heart unfold,
In tranquil light, the world is gold,
A silent love that can't be told.

Gentle moments take their place,
In the calm, I find my grace,
Every worry leaves no trace,
Serenity's sweet embrace.

Time slows down, each tick a sigh,
Thoughts drift like clouds in the sky,
In still waters, dreams float by,
With every breath, I learn to fly.

Nature's hymn resounds within,
A symphony where peace begins,
In its beauty, I will swim,
In quietude, my heart shall brim.

Embraced in moments soft and rare,
Finding solace in the air,
In the hush, there's nothing to compare,
Quietude, my soul's repair.

Secrets Beneath the Surface

Beneath the calm, a world concealed,
Whispers of the past revealed,
In the depths, spirits are healed,
A tapestry of dreams unsealed.

Ripples dance on water's face,
Stories linger in their trace,
Hidden truths, a gentle grace,
In silence, we find our place.

The surface shimmers, yet inside,
Mysteries and secrets hide,
In the stillness, hopes abide,
There's beauty in the tide.

Footprints left on sandy shores,
Echo where the ocean roars,
Each wave shares what nature stores,
In sighs, the heart explores.

Secrets beneath the skies so blue,
In every drop, a story true,
The world whispers, calling you,
To listen deep, to feel anew.

Traces of Unexpressed Emotions

Whispers lost in quiet air,
Heavy hearts, a silent stare.
Words unspoken, left to roam,
In the shadows, far from home.

Fingers brush on empty space,
Searching for a warm embrace.
Silent cries beneath the skin,
Where the truth begins to spin.

Hidden dreams and thoughts concealed,
In the night, they're gently healed.
A flicker deep, a spark ignites,
In the stillness, hidden sights.

Echoes of what might have been,
In the silence, ghosts within.
Colors fade, yet still they stay,
Lingering at the close of day.

All these traces, softly shed,
Of the things we never said.
Wrapped in shadows, soft and tight,
Emotions page, lost from sight.

The Forgotten Melody

Once a song that filled the air,
Notes that danced without a care.
Faded now, as time withdrew,
Echoes lost, a memory few.

Strings of fate, they play along,
In the night, where dreams belong.
Whispers soft, like autumn leaves,
A tale of what the heart believes.

Melodies in twilight speak,
In the silence, sweet but weak.
Footsteps trace an absent beat,
Where the past and present meet.

Underneath the silver moon,
Resonates a silent tune.
Fragments lost in gentle haze,
A haunting of forgotten days.

Yet within each fleeting sound,
Resurgence can perhaps be found.
In the heart, the rhythm swells,
A new song, it softly dwells.

Reflections Amidst the Silence

Mirrors hold the silent gaze,
In their depths, the heart displays.
Fragments of a broken dream,
Caught within a fragile beam.

Stillness wraps the evening tight,
In that space, truths come to light.
Softly spoken, shadows dance,
In the quiet, there's a chance.

Thoughts converge like falling stars,
Tracing lines of hidden scars.
Candle flames flicker and sway,
Guiding souls to find their way.

Within the silence, echoes shine,
With each pulse, the heart aligns.
A reflection lost, now found,
In the stillness, thoughts resound.

Wisdom waits in whispered breath,
In the quiet, life and death.
Trust the silence deep inside,
Where all fears and hopes abide.

Silent Struggles, Unraveled

Within the heart, a storm does churn,
Silent struggles, lessons learned.
Threads of doubt, they twist and weave,
In the shadows where we grieve.

Words like feathers, light as air,
Crushed beneath a weight of care.
Every breath, a measured fight,
In the darkness, seeks the light.

Holding on to whispered dreams,
Fractured hopes and silent screams.
In the depth of night we yearn,
For the flames that always burn.

But in the struggle, strength is born,
In the silence, spirits scorn.
Unraveled threads, they find their way,
In the dawn of a new day.

Every heartbeat marks a choice,
In the stillness, we rejoice.
Through the struggle, we emerge,
With a voice to rise and surge.

Sounds of Solitude

In the stillness of the night,
Whispers dance like gentle light.
Echoes of a fading tune,
Cradled by the silver moon.

Footsteps lost upon the sand,
Carried by the wind's soft hand.
Each breath a sigh, each sigh a dream,
In solitude, we find the theme.

Shadows stretch, their secrets keep,
In silence, worlds awake from sleep.
Stars above begin to gleam,
Resonating with a distant theme.

Mountains hum a quiet song,
Where lonely heartbeats drift along.
Nature's pulse in gentle sway,
Reminds us of the stillness' play.

Here in silence, we belong,
Finding strength in nature's song.
Every note a soothing balm,
In sounds of solitude, we're calm.

Unheard Harmonies

In shadows deep, the music lies,
Wrapped in layers of soft sighs.
Whispers carried on the breeze,
Melodies that bring sweet ease.

A rustling leaf, a distant sound,
Notes that linger, yet unbound.
Between the notes, a space so wide,
Where melodies and silence bide.

Fragrant blooms release their tune,
Crickets chirp beneath the moon.
Unseen choirs call with grace,
In the dark, we find our place.

Every heartbeat, every pause,
Unheard harmonies give cause.
To listen close, to seek the veiled,
In silent realms, our souls are hailed.

Through the stillness, truth reveals,
The unseen music that it feels.
In quiet moments, harmony,
Awaits our ears, our hearts set free.

The Language of Silence

In words unspoken, truths abide,
A soft embrace, a gentle tide.
In silence, meanings intertwine,
Whispers felt, like love divine.

Eyes that speak without a sound,
In sacred space, our hearts are found.
Moments linger, time stands still,
In quietude, we find our will.

Fingers trace the line of grace,
In stillness, we share a space.
The language blooms in subtle flow,
Echoes of what we both know.

Between the laughter, pause and breathe,
In silence, hearts begin to weave.
Stories told in silence' glow,
Reflecting what our souls bestow.

In unison, we learn to feel,
The language of silence is real.
With every glance, and every breath,
In quiet love, we conquer death.

Gentle Awakening

At dawn's first light, the world ignites,
With whispers soft, as day ignites.
Birds awaken, singing sweet,
A symphony where shadows meet.

The dew embraces blades of grass,
Creating gems that softly pass.
Sunbeams stretch with tender grace,
Kissing earth, a warm embrace.

In every rustle, life reborn,
The heart ignites, the spirit's sworn.
With every breath, a brand new chance,
In gentle waking, we advance.

Colors splash across the sky,
As dreams dissolve, we learn to fly.
In soft transitions, hope will glow,
A canvas where new stories flow.

With each moment, beauty flows,
A gentle touch where love bestows.
Awake, alive, the journey starts,
In every breath, we heal our hearts.

Notes from the Void

In shadows deep where whispers dwell,
A silence sings, an ancient bell.
The stars align, a scattered note,
Within the dark, the echoes float.

Through endless stretches, dreams collide,
Each thought a wave; a cosmic tide.
In voids unseen, the truth appears,
With every pulse dissolving fears.

Forgotten tales on stardust trails,
Speak softly where the silence pales.
A journey vast, no map to find,
Yet in this space, we're intertwined.

Voids cradle hopes in fragile light,
As distant worlds ignite the night.
Each flicker tells, a tale we weave,
In silence strong, we learn to believe.

In drifting realms, the heart will yearn,
For notes unheard, the stars still burn.
A symphony from deep inside,
In notes from void, our souls confide.

Serenity's Secrets

In gentle breeze, the leaves do sway,
A tranquil heart, the world at play.
Beneath the stars, our spirits blend,
In quiet peace, where moments mend.

The river's flow, a soft caress,
Whispers of calm, no need to stress.
In twilight's glow, secrets unfold,
As dreams are spun, in threads of gold.

Each little flower sways in time,
A silent prayer, a simple rhyme.
Sun-kissed horizons, soft and bright,
Entwine our souls with pure delight.

The stillness speaks, a soothing balm,
In nature's arms, we find our calm.
With every breath, the worries cease,
Embrace the now, and feel the peace.

In every dawn, a gift to share,
The world awakens, a breath of air.
In serenity's warm embrace,
We find ourselves, our rightful place.

The Quiet that Speaks

In silence, words begin to grow,
A gentle pulse, a softened glow.
The quiet hum reveals the truth,
In stillness found, we find our youth.

When eyes meet eyes, no need for sound,
In echoes rich, the heart is found.
A language felt without a word,
In every glance, our souls are heard.

The whispers of the trees do call,
In quietude, we hear it all.
A faded smile, a knowing glance,
In silence deep, we find our dance.

Time slows down, as moments blend,
In hush of night, the lights descend.
The quiet speaks in gentle ways,
A symphony of soft displays.

In shadows cast, or light imbued,
In simple truth, our hearts renewed.
So let the silence wrap you tight,
In quiet speak, we'll find the light.

Tides of Thought

Waves crash softly on the shore,
Thoughts like tides ebb evermore.
A vast expanse, a swirling sea,
In fluid dreams, we long to be.

Each ripple holds a fleeting sight,
Of memories lost, of pure delight.
In currents strong, our passions flow,
Bringing forth what we might know.

With every wave, a story stirs,
Of whispered hopes and distant murmurs.
The ocean's depth, a canvas wide,
In tides of thought, we freely ride.

As storms arise and calm returns,
In every shift, a lesson learns.
In harmony, we find our place,
In waves of thought, we seek embrace.

So let us dive into the blue,
With open hearts, explore the new.
In tides of thought, forever cast,
We'll sail the seas, our spirits vast.

The Unheard Call of Reality

In shadows deep, the truth resides,
A whisper lost, where silence hides.
In dreams we wander, far away,
Yet reality waits, come what may.

Each heartbeat echoes, a distant plea,
A longing hushed, we struggle to see.
The world unfolds with secrets tight,
In the unseen, lies hidden light.

Through veils of thought, the visions blend,
Moments fleeting, around the bend.
A tapestry woven from light and dark,
In each breath drawn, we find the spark.

The clock ticks softly, time stands still,
In quiet corners, we learn to feel.
With every sigh, the fabric tears,
Unraveling all, in whispered airs.

O, venture forth, into the night,
Embrace the shades, seek the blight.
For in the chaos, clarity calls,
Awaken now, to reality's thralls.

A Palette of Silence

Within the hush, a canvas bare,
Brushstrokes linger, floating in air.
Colors blend with whispers soft,
In silence, dreams begin to loft.

Each hue reflects a hidden thought,
In shades of stillness, life is caught.
A quiet dance, where shadows play,
In strokes of time, we lose our way.

The morning breaks, with light so meek,
Yet in its glow, the silence speaks.
A palette rich, with muted tones,
In every corner, stillness roams.

The echoes fade, yet linger near,
In colors hush, we shed our fear.
For beauty lives in what we hold,
In silent strokes, the heart unfolds.

So take a breath, and paint your dreams,
In quiet moments, life redeems.
A masterpiece of tranquil grace,
In silence found, our sacred space.

The Hidden Terrain

Beneath the surface, secrets lie,
In shadows deep, where spirits sigh.
The earth conceals its ancient scars,
A silent map of forgotten wars.

With every step, a tale unfolds,
In whispered winds, the past retold.
The hidden paths, where few have trod,
In nature's grasp, we search for God.

Unseen valleys, cloaked in mist,
Each stone a witness, a silent twist.
The heart remembers what the eyes cannot,
In hidden terrains, we seek the sought.

To wander through this sacred maze,
Is to embrace the fleeting days.
For in the depths, we find our way,
In hidden terrains, we long to stay.

So tread with care, and listen close,
For in the quiet, wisdom grows.
The land may whisper, the sky may call,
In hidden terrains, we find it all.

In the Depths of Quiet

In stillness lies the world unspun,
Where thoughts and dreams are softly run.
Each breath a wave, a gentle sigh,
In the depths of quiet, we learn to fly.

The heartbeats echo, a rhythm pure,
In moments seized, the soul's allure.
A tranquil space where fears dissolve,
In silence vast, we find resolve.

Beneath the noise, our spirits grow,
In quietude, the wonders flow.
Each whispered hope, a thread of light,
In the depths of quiet, we find our sight.

Embrace the calm, the lull of night,
In every pause, there's hidden flight.
As time unfolds, we hear the call,
In the depths of quiet, we rise and fall.

So let us dwell where whispers reign,
In silent waters, without a chain.
For in that peace, our truth does sprout,
In the depths of quiet, we let it out.

The Quiet Truths We Keep

In whispers shared beneath the stars,
We bury secrets, hidden scars.
With each soft sigh, a tale unfolds,
Of dreams unspoken, hearts consoled.

The world may judge, but we hold tight,
To silent vows and lost delights.
For every truth that goes unseen,
A part of us remains serene.

We walk through life, on paths unknown,
With quiet truths that we have grown.
In shadows cast by fading light,
We find our strength, we find our might.

Each secret held within our chest,
A gentle pause, our hearts at rest.
In quiet corners, love abides,
Where trust and hope become our guides.

So let us cherish what we keep,
The quiet truths, the promises deep.
In every heartbeat, every sigh,
A bond unbroken, you and I.

Hushed Confessions

In twilight's glow, we find our voice,
With hearts laid bare, we make our choice.
To share the burdens, fears that bind,
In hushed confessions, truth defined.

The whispers float on gentle breeze,
Like autumn leaves that dance with ease.
Each word a promise, softly spoken,
An ancient bond that won't be broken.

We harbor dreams, both wild and pure,
In secret places, we ensure.
The courage found in shared belief,
Transforms our pain into relief.

Hushed moments shared beneath the sky,
With every tear, we learn to fly.
Together, we embrace the night,
In hushed confessions, hearts take flight.

So let us linger in this grace,
With whispered truths in this sacred space.
In shadows cast, our souls ignite,
Through hushed confessions, we find light.

Unseen Reflections

In quiet pools where thoughts converge,
We seek the depths where dreams emerge.
With every glance, a story told,
In unseen reflections, hearts unfold.

The mirrors held within our mind,
Reveal the truths we've left behind.
As shadows linger, we reflect,
On paths we've walked, with such respect.

The silence speaks of love and loss,
In every ripple, lines we cross.
With gentle hands, we trace the past,
In unseen reflections, shadows cast.

Through every tear that we have cried,
We find the strength to turn the tide.
In quiet depth, our spirits soar,
Through unseen reflections, we explore.

So as we gaze into the night,
We find the truth in muted light.
In every echo, every sigh,
Unseen reflections never lie.

Shadows of Introspection

In shadows deep, we seek the truth,
In silent moments, we find our youth.
Through whispered thoughts, our minds embrace,
The shadows of introspection's space.

Each flicker of the candle's flame,
Illuminates the heart's own name.
With every heartbeat, doubts collapse,
In shadows soft, the spirit gaps.

We dance with fears that press and pry,
Yet in the stillness, we learn to fly.
Through mirrored visions, we confront,
The shadows of introspection's hunt.

In solitude, we weave our dreams,
With every thought, our courage gleams.
For in the quiet, truths unfold,
In shadows cast, our stories told.

So let us wander, hand in hand,
Through shadows where our hearts withstand.
In every doubt, we find our strength,
In shadows of introspection's length.

Murmurs of the Forgotten

In whispers soft, the echoes flow,
Of lost souls dancing, long ago.
Their secrets linger in the air,
A haunting melody of despair.

In twilight's grasp, the stories fade,
With every sigh, the dreams betrayed.
Forgotten tales, like dust in light,
Yearn for a voice, to break the night.

Shadows linger, memories swirl,
In silent corners, emotions twirl.
Fading faces, shadows of time,
In the stillness, echoes chime.

A broken past, stitched with grace,
Each thread weaves a ghostly trace.
In every heartbeat, truth remains,
Murmurs of love, amidst the pains.

So listen close, to what is not,
For in the silence, wisdom's wrought.
The forgotten sing of lost embraces,
In shadows deep, their spirit graces.

Shadows of Unseen Wisdom

In quiet corners, shadows creep,
Whispered truths, in silence keep.
Veils of twilight, secrets spun,
Unseen wisdom, twilight's sun.

Echoes of ages, softly sway,
Guiding hearts along the way.
In every rustle, every sigh,
Secrets bloom and then pass by.

The weight of knowing, light as air,
Life's mystique, a puzzle rare.
In shadows cast, revelations hide,
Wisdom's grace, forever abide.

An ancient map, through the dark,
Illuminated by a spark.
Seeking paths where shadows play,
Unseen wisdom leads the way.

So heed the whispers in your soul,
Let silence guide you, make you whole.
For in the shadows, truths may gleam,
Unseen wisdom's fragile dream.

The Quiet Within

In the stillness, a heartbeat sings,
The quiet within, solace brings.
Moments linger, soft and bright,
In whispers found, in cloaked light.

Beyond the chaos, peace resides,
Within the heart, where truth abides.
Gentle meadows, softly sigh,
In quietude, we learn to fly.

The world outside may howl and rush,
Yet in our depths, we find that hush.
Calm waters reflect the sky,
In tranquil depths, our spirits fly.

A haven sought, in breath we find,
The quiet within, where love is kind.
It shelters dreams, it nurtures hope,
In still embrace, we learn to cope.

So pause a moment, breathe it in,
Embrace the calm that lies within.
In softest spaces, life reveals,
The quiet within, our heart appeals.

Hushed Confessions

In candlelight, secrets shared,
Hushed confessions of hearts laid bare.
Silent voices, truth unfolds,
In the shadows, life's tales told.

Whispers linger, courage low,
Hidden feelings, soft and slow.
In every glance, a silent plea,
Yearning souls, longing to be free.

Beneath the masks, a world concealed,
In cryptic codes, emotions healed.
The weight of words, so lightly pressed,
Hushed confessions, souls confessed.

A fragile bond, in silence found,
Two beating hearts, in whispers bound.
In sacred trust, the past released,
Hushed confessions, sweetly ceased.

So dare to share the truth you hold,
For in the hush, pure hearts be bold.
In whispered tones, our spirits dance,
Hushed confessions, love's true chance.

Veils of Unuttered Thoughts

In shadows deep where silence dwells,
A whisper lingers, time repels.
Thoughts adrift on quiet streams,
Veils conceal unheard dreams.

Beneath the surface, secrets lie,
A tapestry of endless sighs.
Echoes dance in muted hues,
Veils of thoughts, a cryptic muse.

The heart converses without sound,
In hidden realms, the lost are found.
Within the mind, the fires glow,
Veils of unuttered thoughts bestow.

Threads of longing intertwine,
In unspoken moments, hearts align.
The language wrapped in quiet grace,
Veils of silence, an embrace.

So let the stillness softly weave,
The fragile tales that we believe.
In every pause, a universe sings,
Veils of thoughts and hidden things.

Shrouded Insights

In the twilight where shadows play,
Insights hide, they drift away.
Wrapped in folds of softest night,
Shrouded truths conceal their light.

With every glance, a story waits,
Behind the door of heavy gates.
Glimmers flash in hidden sights,
Whispers soft, shrouded insights.

The heart understanding, yet unsure,
Dancing lightly, searching for more.
In the quiet, meanings blend,
Shrouded thoughts that softly tend.

A veil of mystery cloaked in grace,
In this stillness, find your place.
What's unspoken finds its flights,
Floating free, shrouded insights.

So linger long in shadows cast,
In the unseen, the realm of past.
In every heartbeat, wisdom ignites,
In the dark, shrouded insights.

The Pause Between Words

In the spaces, where silence breathes,
A moment lingers, thought retrieves.
The pause, a canvas, clear and wide,
Between our words, where dreams abide.

It holds a weight we seldom see,
An echo of what's meant to be.
In hesitation, truth unfolds,
The pause between, a tale retolds.

With gentle strength it weaves the air,
An unclaimed gift, a silent prayer.
In every heartbeat, time defines,
The pause between our hidden lines.

So speak in shadows, let it glide,
In whispered tones, let nuance ride.
In every lull, our souls collide,
The pause between, a secret guide.

Embrace the quiet, let it flow,
In every silence, let us grow.
In inner stillness, wisdom stirs,
The pause we keep between our words.

Soft Illuminations

In dim-lit rooms where shadows fold,
Illuminations, soft and bold.
A gentle glow, a tender spark,
Softly brightening the dark.

The light dances on fragile walls,
A quiet echo, beauty calls.
In spaces where the heart can yearn,
Soft illuminations gently burn.

Each corner kissed by tender rays,
Reminds us of forgotten days.
In twilight hues, the spirit lifts,
Softly wrapped in radiant gifts.

A canvas painted with warm light,
In every shade, we find our sight.
The heart ignites, the mind recalls,
Soft illuminations guide our halls.

So let your heart embrace the shine,
In shadows' wake, let love define.
In every glimmer, dreams entwine,
Soft illuminations, pure and fine.

Whispers of the Unspoken

In shadows deep, where silence dwells,
Soft voices rise, but no one tells.
The secrets curl, in twilight's grace,
Unheard they linger, in every space.

Gentle breezes carry dreams,
Unseen threads, like quiet streams.
Each sigh a story, yet untold,
In whispered tones, the heart unfolds.

Through the night, they weave and sway,
A tapestry of lost decay.
In moments hushed, where echoes creep,
The unspoken vows, in silence keep.

So let them dance in moonlit light,
These whispers soft, that take their flight.
For in the stillness, truths shall find,
The fragile threads that bind the mind.

Echoes in the Stillness

The clock ticks slow in dusky glow,
Where shadows play and soft winds blow.
In corners dim, the echoes sigh,
A gentle call that passes by.

Still moments stretch, like twilight's breath,
In quiet realms that dance with death.
Each flickering light, a memory's trace,
Whispers of laughter, in time's embrace.

The world outside may rush and race,
But here we find a sacred space.
Each heartbeat lands like softest rain,
In echoes sweet, we find our pain.

What once was lost in noise and strife,
Now hums a tune, of quiet life.
In stillness profound, we recognize,
The echoes rise, like morning skies.

Secrets Beneath the Surface

In waters deep where shadows glide,
The secrets dwell, they cannot hide.
Beneath the waves, a world unseen,
Where whispers linger, calm and serene.

The surface glimmers with light's embrace,
Yet below, there hides a quieter place.
Each ripple holds a tale of old,
Of treasures lost, and dreams untold.

The curious fish swim fast and free,
Unraveling knots of mystery.
While currents pull with gentle hands,
The stories flow like shifting sands.

So dive into the depths of thought,
Where secrets bloom and fears are caught.
For in the silence, truths emerge,
Beneath the surface, we find the urge.

Murmurs of the Heart

In quiet moments, feelings stir,
A melody soft, like wings of a fir.
Each thud a note, so tender and frail,
A whisper escaping, a soft, sweet wail.

Through pathways worn, where shadows tread,
The murmurs rise, both spoken and said.
They dance in circles, they swirl and weave,
Crafting a tapestry, hearts believe.

With every beat, a story flows,
In twilight's hush, the warmth it shows.
The love that lingers, the pain that stings,
In murmurs soft, the heart still sings.

So let them echo, these sounds divine,
For in their chorus, we intertwine.
In gentle whispers, we choose to find,
The murmurs of love that heal the mind.

Soft Rays of Revelation

In the morning light so soft,
Whispers dance on petals bright.
Dreams awaken, shadows flee,
Nature's grace, the soul's delight.

Golden beams through branches stream,
Kissing dew on grass so green.
Every glance, a new connection,
In this world, we find our sheen.

Fleeting clouds drift in the sky,
As the day begins to bloom.
All around, the vibrant life,
Fades away our darkest gloom.

Moments linger, hearts expand,
Time slows down, we breathe it in.
Every ray, a warm embrace,
Revealing truths that lie within.

So let us bask in twilight's glow,
With every breath, the spirit thrives.
Soft rays of revelation shine,
In these moments, love arrives.

The Subtle Shift

The world tilts, a gentle sway,
Silent whispers in the air.
Change is coming, soft as night,
Awareness tinged with quiet care.

Footsteps linger on the path,
Tread lightly where the heart explores.
Little notes, a shifting breeze,
Witness life as it restores.

Colors blend, the dawn transforms,
Life unfolds in tender seams.
With every heartbeat, something stirs,
In the stillness, fleeting dreams.

Like a painter with a brush,
Strokes of fate, a dance of chance.
We adapt, we bend, we grow,
In this realm, we take our stance.

Embrace the subtle, heed the signs,
In the chaos, find the truth.
For the shift is but a moment,
Guiding us back to our roots.

Moments of Clarity

In the noise, a sudden calm,
Thoughts align like stars at night.
Sifting through the tangled minds,
Glimmers spark, our spirits light.

A breath taken, and then we see,
What once was lost now falls in place.
The world unveils its hidden paths,
Each step forward, full of grace.

Truth emerges, unclouded skies,
Answers whisper, soft yet clear.
Each insight, a guiding star,
Leading forward, dispelling fear.

Fragments of our lives align,
Mosaic pieces, time revealed.
With every moment, clarity grows,
The essence of the heart unsealed.

So cherish these bright moments found,
In the stillness, wisdom flows.
As fragments turn to whole anew,
Moments of clarity bestows.

An Ode to Silence

In the hush of early morn,
When the world is bathed in peace.
Silence sings a gentle song,
Offering hearts a sweet release.

No clamor breaks the tranquil air,
Each breath becomes a sacred prayer.
The mind drifts softly, free as clouds,
In silence, we find solace rare.

Echoes fade, the spirit breathes,
In the stillness, pathways green.
Wisdom waits in quiet shade,
In silence, we learn what is seen.

Time surrenders to the calm,
Moments stretch like open sea.
An ode to silence, pure and true,
Where we become who we're meant to be.

Reverberations of the heart,
Whisper secrets, soft and clear.
In this space, all burdens cease,
An ode to silence, ever near.

The Whispering Depths

In shadows deep where secrets dwell,
A quiet voice begins to swell.
It calls to hearts that seek to know,
The stories woven in the flow.

Beneath the waves, a tranquil sigh,
Nature's pulse will never lie.
Each echo paints a vibrant quest,
For in the depths, we find our rest.

Soft melodies of water's grace,
Lead wandering souls to find their place.
In every ripple, life unfolds,
The truth in whispers yet untold.

As night descends, the stars ignite,
Guiding us through the velvet night.
In twilight's glow, we feel the trust,
That binds our dreams with cosmic dust.

The depths remind us of our ties,
To earth, to sky, and endless ties.
With every breath, we dive anew,
In whispered depths, our spirits flew.

Time in Stillness

In moments paused, we find the space,
To taste the stillness, feel its grace.
Each second stretches, bends like light,
A canvas blank, a starry night.

The ticking clock begins to fade,
As thoughts unwind and dreams invade.
A breath held close, the world attunes,
To whispers soft of silent moons.

In quiet corners, peace abounds,
A sanctuary where hope surrounds.
We linger long, we learn to be,
In time's embrace, we are set free.

With gentle hands, we shape the hour,
Finding strength in nature's power.
The clock may tick, yet here we stand,
Forever lost within this land.

Time drifts like leaves on autumn's breeze,
In stillness found, our souls find ease.
Each fleeting moment, richly spun,
In sacred silence, we are one.

The Elusive Understanding

Beneath the veil of thought's embrace,
Lies knowledge chased, a timeless race.
With questions deep, we seek to find,
That fleeting truth that lingers blind.

A puzzle crafted, piece by piece,
In riddles spun, our minds release.
Yet answers hide in shadows cast,
Elusive threads, they fade so fast.

In every glance, a story stirs,
A world of whispers, silent blurs.
We dance with doubt, we hold the key,
To understand what cannot be.

With patience worn and hearts displayed,
We venture forth, though often swayed.
The mind's pursuit, a winding road,
Each step we take, a heavy load.

Yet in the struggle, beauty blooms,
For understanding's light consumes.
In every question, truth we find,
Elusive still, yet intertwined.

The Dance of Quiet Moments

In twilight's glow, the shadows play,
A waltz unfolds at end of day.
The gentle breeze, it lifts and sways,
In quiet moments, life displays.

With every sigh, the world stands still,
A dance of hearts, a soulful thrill.
In whispered tones, we lose control,
Embracing time, it feeds the soul.

The rustling leaves, a soft refrain,
Nature's anthem in sweet gain.
Each heartbeat echoes in the air,
A rhythm found, beyond compare.

As stars emerge, the night inspires,
Awakening our soft desires.
With every glance, connections weave,
In quiet moments, we believe.

A sacred space where dreams align,
A tapestry of moments entwined.
In every breath, the dance extends,
In quiet joys, our spirit mends.

Brewing Thoughts

In the silence of the morn,
Ideas begin to churn,
Like coffee brewing slow,
From dark to light they'll turn.

Whispers float upon the air,
As visions start to form,
Each thought a little spark,
In creative chaos warm.

A gentle hum begins to rise,
Within the mind's embrace,
Where dreams collide and blend,
In a harmonious space.

With every sip of time spent here,
New worlds begin to grow,
Through courage and through fears,
As seeds of thought we sow.

So let the moments linger long,
In this sacred brew,
For in the heart of silence,
Our greatest truths break through.

Secrets Carried by the Breeze

The wind whispers secrets low,
As it dances through the trees,
Carrying tales from afar,
On wings of gentle ease.

It knows of hearts that ache,
And dreams that slip away,
Of whispered hopes and fears,
That in twilight fade to gray.

Through the rustling leaves it sighs,
A melody of the night,
Each note an echo of the past,
Softly fading out of sight.

The breeze wraps around our souls,
A comforting embrace,
It holds our truths and longings,
And sweeps them into space.

So listen close to the gentle air,
For in it, secrets swirl,
The stories of the universe,
In every dance and twirl.

The Midnight Whisper

When the clock strikes midnight's call,
And shadows stretch and sway,
A whisper rides the silent air,
Inviting dreams to play.

Beneath the moon's soft, watchful gaze,
The world begins to pause,
As time unveils its hidden truths,
And speaks without a cause.

In the quiet of the night,
Thoughts begin to roam,
Across the fabric of the dark,
In search of a true home.

Each sigh, each breath, each gentle thought,
Is wrapped in starlit grace,
In the stillness of the hour,
We find our rightful place.

So cherish those whispers of the night,
For they carry deep delight,
With each hidden promise shared,
Underneath the silver light.

Strains in the Quiet

In the quiet of the shut door,
A tension hangs so light,
Strains of life unspoken,
Waiting for the bright.

The silence swells with meaning,
As shadows softly dance,
Inviting all those whispered thoughts,
To join the silent trance.

Each heartbeat echoes softly,
In the laid-back retreat,
While dreams unspool and linger,
On hastily made sheets.

Yet in that hushed communion,
The struggle finds its sound,
Strains of hope and yearning loud,
In the peace, they abound.

So let the quiet tell its tale,
In the stillness shared,
For even in the silence deep,
A symphony is bared.

Voices Beneath Still Waters

Beneath the surface, whispers flow,
Secrets linger in the undertow.
Echoes dance in the silent deep,
Carried by currents, they softly creep.

Ripples form from a wordless song,
Where time is still, yet feelings long.
In the depths, the shadows play,
Their silent tales drift far away.

Moonlit beams touch the hidden heart,
Revealing truths that never part.
In stillness, voices softly blend,
A symphony that will not end.

Listen close; the water knows,
The language of the ebb and flows.
Each movement is a word unsaid,
A story told where dreams have led.

Though silence reigns upon the lake,
The waters listen, the spirits wake.
All that glimmers hides within,
A world alive beneath the skin.

The Calm Before Understanding

In the hush before the storm rolls in,
Where doubts gather, hearts begin.
Clouds hang low, yet skies hold still,
A tranquil space where hopes can fill.

The quiet breath holds deep allure,
Awakening thoughts, both raw and pure.
In this pause, wisdom takes its place,
Unraveling dreams with gentle grace.

Morning light peeks through the grey,
Illuminating paths each way.
A flicker of truth begins to rise,
Veils of uncertainty start to die.

In stillness, vision comes alive,
As spirits gather, thrive and strive.
From the calm, we start to learn,
With every heartbeat, the flames will burn.

Questions linger, answers near,
In this moment, we confront our fear.
The calm before, a sacred space,
Fostering understanding's embrace.

Unspoken Dreams

In shadows cast by fading light,
Dreams lie silent, out of sight.
Whispers linger in the night air,
Hopes on the edge, laid bare.

Crimson skies greet the dawning day,
Yet fears often lead the way.
In the hush, ambitions fade,
Yearning hearts in silence laid.

In every sigh, a story starts,
Unvoiced wishes fill our hearts.
Like stars that shimmer in the dark,
Each dream holds an embered spark.

With courage gathered, shall we speak?
The path to truth may feel quite bleak.
But in those words, the light will glow,
Igniting dreams, allowing flow.

Let tongues unfasten, let voices ring,
In harmony, our spirits sing.
For unspoken dreams, once inside,
Shall take their flight, no longer hide.

The Softest Truths

In gentle whispers, truths reside,
Beneath the surface, we confide.
Each word, a feather, light and free,
Carried softly, just you and me.

Unraveled tales in the quiet night,
Where shadows dance with soft moonlight.
In the stillness, hearts combine,
Mending fractures through the line.

Fragile hopes bloom in tender care,
The softest truths we bravely share.
In vulnerability, we trust,
Finding strength, as all souls must.

Like petals falling, released with grace,
Our honest words find their place.
Each truth a thread in the weave of fate,
Binding us close, transforming state.

Through gentle tones, we learn to see,
The beauty of our shared decree.
In softest truths, love's light appears,
Easing burdens, calming fears.

The Solitude of Illumination

In quiet corners, shadows play,
A light that flickers, then fades away.
Whispers linger in silent air,
Solitude breathes, a gentle care.

Stars blink softly, a distant song,
In moments still, where we belong.
Lonely thoughts begin to weave,
In this refuge, we believe.

The glow of dawn, a tender trace,
Illumination in a secluded space.
Every heartbeat, a whispered thought,
In solitude, the lessons sought.

Forgotten dreams begin to rise,
Underneath the expansive skies.
With every flicker, truth is found,
In solitude, where hope abounds.

So let the shadows dance and twine,
In this stillness, the light will shine.
For in the night, we reclaim our right,
To embrace the solitude of light.

Echoes of the Unheard

Beneath the layers of time and space,
Whispers linger without a trace.
The echoes call from far away,
Remnants of voices lost in gray.

In the silence where secrets lie,
Words unspoken begin to fly.
Like shadows dancing on the wall,
They weave through air, a haunting call.

The heart remembers what ears can't hear,
In the stillness, the truth feels near.
Gentle murmurs in the night,
Woven threads of lost delight.

Each echo carries a weighty tale,
Of joy and sorrow that will not pale.
Through whispered dreams and faded light,
Unseen stories take their flight.

So listen close to the quiet sound,
For in the hush, the lost are found.
The echoes of the unheard remain,
A symphony of joy and pain.

The Weight of a Whisper

In the quiet of the twilight hour,
Whispers drift like petals, a flower.
Softly spoken, they carry weight,
A gentle truth that cannot wait.

Each word a feather, light and free,
Yet grounded in the heart's decree.
A hush surrounds the fragile sound,
In whispers, our souls abound.

Secrets tucked within a sigh,
Echoes linger as they pass by.
For vulnerability wears a crown,
In whispered tones, we let them drown.

The weight we carry, both sharp and sweet,
In every whisper, life's heartbeat.
Fragile threads, an unseen guide,
Leading us where our truths reside.

So listen close as shadows blend,
In whispers lies the heart's true friend.
For each soft word can still ignite,
The weight of every hidden light.

Beneath the Velvet Night

Underneath the velvet sky,
Stars are scattered, nearby, awry.
The moon whispers in silken light,
As dreams take flight into the night.

Gentle breezes, soft and mild,
Embrace the earth as night beguiled.
With every sigh, the world breathes slow,
In stillness, our emotions flow.

Shadows stretch in the silver glow,
Touching secrets we long to know.
A canvas painted with dusk and dawn,
Where hearts awaken, a new song.

Time stands still in this twilight grace,
With every breath, we find our place.
Beneath the sky, we cast our fears,
In velvet night, the soul appears.

So let us wander through this dream,
Where every star holds a silent theme.
Beneath the velvet night, we see,
The beauty in our mystery.

The Language of Silence

In shadows deep, where whispers dwell,
Words unsaid weave a hidden spell.
The heart speaks soft, in pauses clear,
Embracing truth that draws us near.

In quiet moments, spirits dance,
A gaze exchanged, a fleeting chance.
Silence holds what voices lack,
A gentle strength that won't turn back.

Each breath a bond, more than we see,
In silence shared, we dare to be.
Unknown stories linger in the air,
In stillness bright, we find what's rare.

The world outside may loudly clash,
But here we find a sacred stash.
In whispers low, the soul takes flight,
The language found in stars and night.

So let us seek the quiet space,
Where silence speaks in its embrace.
For in this hush, the truth ignites,
The language of silence, pure delights.

Sounds of Hidden Depths

Beneath the waves where secrets play,
Echoes linger, drifting away.
Each ripple holds a tales untold,
In depths of blue, the heart turns bold.

The whispers of the ocean's song,
Unravel mysteries, deep and long.
With every tide that ebbs and flows,
Sounds of hidden depths gently rose.

In caverns dark, the sirens call,
A melody that swells and falls.
Each drop of water, voice in flight,
In swimming thoughts, we find our light.

The sea holds notes of joy and strife,
In harmony, it breathes with life.
Listen closely, let the heart lend,
To sounds of depths, our souls ascend.

With every wave that breaks the shore,
Echoes linger, whispering more.
A symphony beneath the foam,
In hidden depths, we come back home.

Stillness Unfolded

In the quiet of the early morn,
Where dreams dissolve, and hopes are born.
Each moment breathes a delicate grace,
In stillness, time finds its rightful place.

The world holds its breath, awaiting light,
As shadows linger, fading from sight.
In gentle pauses, life reveals,
The beauty found in what it feels.

Like petals drifting on a stream,
Soft whispers float, a muted dream.
In peaceful corners, souls unite,
In stillness unfolded, hearts take flight.

The air is thick with thoughts unspoken,
In silent spaces, sweet bonds are woven.
Embrace the hush, let worries cease,
In stillness, we find our inner peace.

For within the calm, we meet ourselves,
In every heartbeat, a story dwells.
So let the silence cradle you tight,
In stillness unfolded, we find our light.

Beneath the Calm Waters

Underneath where sunlight glows,
Life unfolds in softest flows.
Beneath the calm, there lies a dance,
In hidden realms, we take our chance.

With every flicker, shadows play,
In waters deep, they find their way.
Secrets whisper in liquid sighs,
Beneath the calm, where silence lies.

The stillness hides a world so vast,
In tranquil depths, we hold the past.
Each ripple tells a tale of grace,
Beneath the calm, we find our place.

Where currents weave and dreams collide,
In quiet depths, our thoughts confide.
With open hearts, we brave the seas,
Beneath the calm, the spirit frees.

So dive into the serene embrace,
Where hidden waters find their space.
For in the depths, we grow and rise,
Beneath the calm, the heart unties.

Lullabies of the Mind

Whispers dance on the breeze,
Softly cradling dreams to sleep.
The stars blink in gentle ease,
While the night begins to creep.

Thoughts entwine like vines in shade,
Wrapping secrets in their hold.
A silent serenade,
As the heart whispers bold.

Clouds drift through a velvet sky,
Each one carries a sigh's tune.
In the stillness, we rely,
On the song of the moon.

Echos of the day's retreat,
Fade into the night's embrace.
In this calm, our souls find heat,
In the quiet's tender space.

With each breath, the world dissolves,
Into slumber's soft delight.
In the silence, love resolves,
Sailing gently through the night.

Reflections in a Still Lake

Mirrored skies in water's glass,
Hold secrets in their embrace.
Gentle ripples slowly pass,
Each one leaves a trace of grace.

Trees bow low to kiss the shore,
Whispering their silent tales.
Nature's breath forevermore,
Filling hearts with soothing gales.

Colors bleed at dusk's sweet tune,
Painting shadows on the ground.
In the glow of silver moon,
Peace and solace can be found.

Time stands still, a fleeting glance,
As we gather dreams while they last.
Life unfolds in quiet dance,
Reflecting memories amassed.

In the lake's enchanting hold,
Truths and wonders intertwine.
Through its depths, we unfold,
The beauty of the divine.

The Soft Footsteps of Insight

Quiet whispers in the mind,
Gently tracing paths anew.
In the stillness, we can find,
Wisdom hidden from our view.

Each step taken, slow and sure,
Brings the light from deep within.
In the silence, hearts endure,
Opening where thoughts begin.

Revelations softly call,
Like soft winds across the plain.
In their echoes, we stand tall,
Learning from both loss and gain.

Steps of courage lead the way,
Through the fog, the shadows play.
As we wander, night fades gray,
Insight guides us towards the day.

With each moment, depths expand,
Truths arise like morning sun.
In the stillness, we will stand,
Knowing all we've just begun.

Truths in the Shadows

In the corners, secrets dwell,
Whispers curling in the air.
Softly ringing like a bell,
Truths await, both dark and rare.

Every shadow tells a tale,
Of the light and depths we fear.
Listen close; let doubts curtail,
For the heart will always steer.

Hidden depths in twilight's glow,
Guide the way through restless night.
In the stillness, wisdom flows,
Sparks of clarity ignite.

Find the balance, light and dark,
Both together shape our fate.
In their dance, we leave a mark,
Learning love can compensate.

So we tread with careful grace,
Through the mysteries that bind.
In each secret, find your space,
For the truths are intertwined.

The Unseen Lament

Whispers weave through shadows cast,
Silent cries from ages past.
Their echoes haunt the empty night,
As stars forget to shine their light.

Longing weeps in hidden souls,
Yearning hearts, like restless shoals.
Within the dark, a story stays,
In muted tones, the spirit sways.

Memories dance on fragile threads,
In silence, where the sorrow spreads.
The unseen tear meets the moon's glow,
A lament shared with the winds that blow.

Glimmers spark in sorrow's flight,
A gentle hand to hold the night.
The unseen burden starts to heal,
In quiet moments, we reveal.

Together we can face the dawn,
In strength that's built from what is gone.
Embrace the loss, let shadows blend,
For in the end, we learn to mend.

In the Quietude of Thought

Beneath the weight of whispered dreams,
The silence shimmers, softly beams.
In stillness found, the mind can flow,
As secrets of the heart bestow.

Thoughts align in gentle grace,
In quietude, we find our place.
A moment held, as time stands still,
To ponder wishes, quiet will.

Reflections pool in tranquil minds,
As clarity in peace unwinds.
A canvas blank, pure and serene,
Revealing paths yet to be seen.

In gentle waves, our visions rise,
Soft echoes of the soul's surprise.
For in the quiet, wisdom wakes,
An endless journey, silence takes.

Through whispered thoughts, we bravely tread,
In worlds imagined, hopes are spread.
An inner light begins to shine,
As quietude reveals the divine.

Tranquil Insights

Beneath the trees where shadows lie,
Soft whispers drift and gently sigh.
In nature's heart, we find our peace,
A world of calm, our minds release.

The gentle rustle of the leaves,
Carries thoughts where the spirit weaves.
Each moment holds a truth so clear,
In tranquil spaces, free from fear.

Mountains stand with wisdom grand,
While rivers flow, a guiding hand.
In sunsets rich with golden beams,
The universe cradles our dreams.

As moonlight bathes the quiet night,
We gather strength from silver light.
In stillness found, we close our eyes,
And breathe the dreams that softly rise.

Here in this peace, we find our way,
Through tranquil insights, night and day.
The heart, a compass, shows its course,
In harmony, we find our source.

Still Waters Run Deep

The mirror holds the moon's soft glow,
A depth concealed, a quiet flow.
In mirrored realms, reflections play,
Where stillness holds the words we say.

Beneath the calm, the currents sway,
A dance of thoughts that rarely stray.
In silence, ripples touch the core,
Whispers carried from the shore.

Life's secrets murmur, softly steep,
In layers deep, the soul will creep.
Each hidden truth, a tale to tell,
In waters still, we know so well.

As shadows blend with dawn's first light,
We find the courage in the night.
For deep within, the heart will leap,
Embracing all, where still waters keep.

In peace, we tread through life's great sea,
With gentle hearts, we learn to be.
Embracing all, we seek, we sow,
For still waters run deep, and so.

Secrets Wrapped in Stillness

In shadows deep where silence weaves,
The secrets sleep, like autumn leaves.
A breath held tight in evening's glow,
They murmur low, where few will go.

The hush enfolds all whispered dreams,
In quiet streams, the soft moonbeams.
A dance of thoughts, both old and new,
In stillness, they blossom, take their cue.

As night unveils its velvet skies,
Hidden truths reveal their guise.
A sacred trust in velvet night,
Wrapped in the still, they take to flight.

Each secret hush, a tale untold,
In silence bold, the heart unfolds.
Embrace the pause, let echoes ring,
In stillness, find what whispers bring.

The world may rush, yet here I stay,
In secret play, come what may.
With open ears, I choose to hear,
The stillness speaks, and I draw near.

Beneath the Surface of Noise

Amidst the clamor, where chaos sings,
The heart still knows the peace it brings.
A truth concealed in daily strife,
Beneath the waves, a deeper life.

Voices clash like thunder's roar,
Yet softly knocks another door.
Resonant peace in swells and sways,
Beyond the noise, a calm array.

Listen close, the whispers say,
In still waters, thoughts may play.
A lullaby beneath the din,
Where quiet realms begin to spin.

Waves may rise and fall with haste,
But time reveals the subtle taste.
In every roar, a hidden grace,
A space of quiet, a sacred place.

In the heart, a river flows,
Beneath the rush, the stillness grows.
In every sound, a secret lies,
A tranquil truth beyond the cries.

The Quiet Revelation

In moments still, the soul can breathe,
Where silence weaves, and doubts relieve.
Awakening in soft embrace,
The quiet reveals its gentle grace.

In whispered thoughts, the light unfolds,
A tapestry of dreams retold.
With eyes closed tight, I see the glow,
In silence found, the truth will show.

The dawn breaks slow; the world is new,
In whispers soft, the heart breaks through.
A revelation learned in time,
In quiet words, a silent rhyme.

Each day begins with hope's own light,
In gentle beams, both warm and bright.
As dreams emerge from shades of grey,
The quiet speaks, and I obey.

In every pause, a story lives,
The heart's own voice, the stillness gives.
A quiet truth, a gem bestowed,
In silence, love's own path is showed.

Whispers of the Heart

In tender beats, a murmur stirs,
The heart reveals what silence prefers.
Through shadows cast, in vibrant hues,
A whisper sings, a love ensues.

Each pulse a song, each breath a thread,
In quietude, where dreams are fed.
With every word, the soul connects,
In whispered vows, the heart reflects.

In secret places, thoughts entwine,
A sacred space where hearts align.
Like gentle waves that kiss the shore,
The whispers call, they ask for more.

In silence wrapped, emotions bloom,
Transforming shadows, banishing gloom.
With open hearts, we dare to leap,
In whispered hopes, our truths we keep.

Beneath the stars, a pact we share,
In whispered dreams, we find our care.
A language soft, a bond so sweet,
In gentle whispers, our hearts meet.

Lingering Solitude

In the quiet corners of my mind,
Thoughts weave like shadows in the light.
Each breath a whisper, soft and kind,
In solitude's embrace, I find my sight.

The clock ticks slowly, marking time,
Yet here I linger, lost in dreams.
A gentle rhythm, a silent rhyme,
In silence, I hear the heart's soft streams.

Windows open to the night so vast,
Stars twinkle like secrets left untold.
Moments fade, but memories last,
In this solitude, my soul unfolds.

A single candle burns bright and low,
Its flickering flame dances in the haze.
In stillness, I learn what I can't show,
To cherish each word, lost in a haze.

Embracing shadows with open arms,
I wade through thoughts, both dark and fair.
Lingering solitude holds its charms,
In this sacred space, I find my prayer.

Echoing in the Dark

In the chamber where silence dwells,
Echoes of voices softly play.
Whispers of secrets, forgotten spells,
In dark, they twist and sway.

Footsteps linger on the cold stone,
Past burdens carried, heavy and stark.
In quiet moments, I feel alone,
With shadows dancing, leaving a mark.

A heartbeat echoes, a pulse of fear,
Cries of the lost, calling my name.
Yet there is hope, lingering near,
In the dark, I fan the flame.

Moonlight filters through broken glass,
Casting dreams in a silver sheen.
I face the truth, let memories pass,
In the dark, life feels serene.

Embracing the void, the silence sings,
In shadows where my spirit sparks.
Echoes remind me of fragile things,
In this embrace of endless dark.

The Subtle Art of Listening

In the stillness, a symphony plays,
Notes of life dance through the air.
In each pause, the heart's truth lays,
A gentle touch, a whispered care.

Birds in flight share stories long,
Leaves rustle like secrets unspun.
Listening closely, I join the song,
In nature's chorus, I am one.

The rustling wind, a lover's sigh,
Each word unspoken, a hidden tale.
Beneath the surface where feelings lie,
In quiet moments, intuition prevails.

Voices mingle, rise and fall,
In crowded rooms, a world apart.
Yet in the silence, I hear it all,
The subtle art of an open heart.

To listen deeply, to understand,
To weave connections, both near and far.
In every heartbeat, in every hand,
The subtle art shines like a star.

Breath of the Unheard

In shadows cast by whispered dreams,
The unheard voices softly breathe.
Silent stories flow like streams,
In this stillness, I believe.

Through cracked walls, young hopes arise,
Filling the void with gentle grace.
In every sigh, a truth that lies,
Longing to find its rightful place.

The breeze carries a tale untold,
In each rustle, a heart's soft plea.
Courage breathes where fears take hold,
In silence, we learn to be free.

Understanding swells like the tide,
Washing away the weight of despair.
With every breath, a balance inside,
In the unheard, we find our share.

In quietude, our spirits soar,
Listening closely to what we feel.
In the breath of the unheard, we explore,
The silent truths that heal and reveal.

The Hidden Path

In shadows deep, a trail unfolds,
Whispers beckon, secrets hold.
Leaves rustle softly underfoot,
Nature's song, a quiet root.

With every step, the world grows small,
A hidden path, a beckoning call.
Sunlight dances through the trees,
A gentle guide on the evening breeze.

Mysteries linger in the air,
Each turn reveals a truth laid bare.
Footprints fade on the forest floor,
Yet the spirit longs to explore.

Voices echo, ancient and wise,
Leading hearts to the starry skies.
Lost in moments, found in grace,
On the hidden path, we find our place.

In Silence, I Discover

In quietude, my thoughts will flow,
A deeper self begins to show.
The noise of life, a distant hum,
In silence, truth's sweet whisper comes.

Moments pause, the world stands still,
Time unfolds, a gentle thrill.
I breathe in deep, let worries fade,
In silence, I'm no longer afraid.

Lessons born from stillness deep,
The heart finds peace, the soul to keep.
Within the calm, new visions start,
In silence, I engage my heart.

With every breath, my spirit grows,
In stillness, wisdom softly glows.
Each subtle sigh, a gift divine,
In silence, I begin to shine.

Quiet Murmurs of Wisdom

In gentle tones, the whispers spread,
A tale of thoughts, of hearts well-read.
Mountains echo with ancient lore,
Quiet murmurs draw me to explore.

Through nature's voice, the truth appears,
A language spoken through the years.
The brook sings softly, trees reply,
In quiet murmurs, the wisdom lies.

Life's lessons held in drops of dew,
In stillness, I perceive what's true.
A guiding light in shadows cast,
In each small whisper, lessons vast.

The stars above, a cosmic guide,
Throughout the silence, dreams collide.
In every heart, a sacred space,
Quiet murmurs reveal love's grace.

Unveiling the Unspoken

In silence thick, we often dwell,
Words unvoiced, a story to tell.
Eyes that meet, a spark ignites,
Unveiling truths in the shadowed lights.

Emotions dance upon the tongue,
In glances shared, old songs are sung.
The heartbeats sync, a tender thread,
Connections bloom where words have fled.

In every pause, a promise grows,
In unsaid things, our spirit knows.
Through the silence, we can see,
Unveiling what we're meant to be.

With gentle hands, we touch the air,
Unspoken bonds, a precious layer.
Together lost in what is shared,
In the quiet, we are bared.

9 781805 609490